Jared Barhite

Our Profession

And Other Poems

Jared Barhite

Our Profession
And Other Poems

ISBN/EAN: 9783744705134

Printed in Europe, USA, Canada, Australia, Japan

Cover: Foto ©Thomas Meinert / pixelio.de

More available books at **www.hansebooks.com**

OUR PROFESSION

AND

OTHER POEMS.

BY

JARED BARHITE,

PRINCIPAL OF THIRD WARD GRAMMAR SCHOOL,
LONG ISLAND CITY, N. Y.

PUBLISHED BY

WILLIAM E. BARHITE,

270 Freeman Avenue, Long Island City, N. Y.

1895.

PREFACE.

During the past quarter of a century, it has been a pleasant pastime for me to obey the dictates of my feelings and inscribe them upon paper.

The present volume is a collection of these vagrant pastimes, some of which have wandered far, while others have never before appeared to any eye save the writer's.

To call them home, introduce them to each other, and properly house them, seems a parental duty.

If in them there is a thought that shall inspire others of my profession to feel the dignity and responsibility of the calling, their publication will not have been in vain.

The intent being good, the fruit cannot be evil.

THE AUTHOR.

DEDICATION.

The true end of life is to elevate man
In body, in mind, and in spirit,
That here he may serve some beneficent plan,
Then a mansion in heaven inherit.

INDEX.

INDEX.

INDEX.

INVOCATION TO THE MUSE.

DIDACTIC muse Calliope,
    Expand thy soothing silent wings,
Touch chords of measured harmony
Wherein the soul ecstatic sings,
Let language fraught with living truth
Find such expression by thy art,
As shall assist the guides of youth
To fire the soul and win the heart.

Remove the barriers which so long
Have held in thraldom many a mind,
Sing to the deaf a ransom-song,
Be eyes to those whose souls are blind ;
Teach those who mould the plastic mind
To know that God hath never given
A mission weightier, more refined,
To angels round the courts of heaven,
Than that of training human minds
Committed unto human hands,
In which the spirit e'er survives
And through eternity expands.

Paint truthfully the living dead
Whose sensibilities were slain
By tyros, oft unskilled, unread,   .
In all the workings of the brain;
Whose concepts of the avenues
That reach the mind of tender youth,
Are labyrinths of tangled views
Devoid of art, science, and truth;
Touch but that chord of magic power
Which gives the soul augmented bliss,
And lifts it for the present hour
Above the world's base selfishness;
Then let the search-light of the soul
Illumine every page that's read,
Until an animated whole
Shall supersede the living dead.

Then, then shall dawn the golden day
When Ignorance shall shamed-faced fly.
Before the potent living ray
Of mind, touched by effulgency
That pours its light in vital force,
Upon the mind of plastic youth,
And leads it gently to the source
Of light and scientific truth.

OUR PROFESSION.

There's an art in our profession,
Which cannot be wholly learned
From all books in our possession,
Though their leaves be deftly turned
Till the mind shall grasp the meaning
Of each truth they may contain,
Yet there remains a gleaning
Not a product of the brain.

One may know the truths of science
Till his mind may have full store,
Or may place some great reliance
On ancient and modern lore;
He may count the stars in heaven,
He may trace them in their course,
And from data that is given
He may prove creation's source;
He may use the best of diction
To portray his studied thought;
He may draw from truth and fiction
All the charm with which they're fraught;
He may be a friend of Nature
And may understand her laws;
He may prove embryo creature
Has within itself a "cause";
He may fathom all creation

And dwell among the stars,
Visit every land and nation
And return with honor's scars;
Yet he may lack a power,—
Occult to scientific truth—
Which is Heaven's richest dower
To the guides of ardent youth.

Though all these may give a polish
To the gem that lights the soul,
They are weak, useless, and foolish,
When they're taken for the whole
Of all the powers required
To entrance the youthful mind,
With a spirit so inspired
As to touch the eyes of blind
With a bright illumination
That shall prove itself to be
More than a corruscation
Of a short-lived ecstasy.

By intuition, children know
A heart that cares for them;
They recognize a friend or foe,
At instantaneous ken.
No mask can shield a fraud or fool,
E'en from a puerile mind;
It knows by rules not learned at school
The way true hearts to find.
An earnest love, unbounded, firm,—

A God-gift from our birth—
By far outweighs the noblest charm
Can be acquired on earth.

Who has not drunk deep at the well
Of childhood's innocence,
Or thinks that he should ever dwell
At such an eminence,
That he can never bend to raise
And cheer a longing heart,
Will waste his precious hours and days,
And finally depart
Without such fruitage or reward
As ever should be given
To him, who serves master or Lord,
And hopes for bliss in heaven.

Who sees no soul-buds here expand
To blossom by and by,
Hath fathomed not the great command
For which we live and die.
The State demands that every son
And daughter shall be free
From ignorance and vice which run
Toward crime and misery.
The future of our noble State
Dwells now in plastic form;
If she her past would emulate
And meet the coming storm
Of chaos, whose portentous wing

Seems hovering not afar,
In every school-room we should sing
Of banner and of star
That gave the land to Liberty,
And with a bold huzza
Proclaim that he who would be free
Must honor right and law.

Who serves his State and fellow-man
And plies his skill at best,
Assists to carry out the plan
To make all truly blest;
He may not sit in marble hall
Where legislators meet,
Nor may he rear fine towers tall,
Or dwell in a retreat
Where monks and nuns with solemn prayer
Pour out their orison;
The test of faith is filial care,
And duty nobly done.
Minds let us mould, men may we rear,
For God, for State, for man,
Using the right without a fear
To mar the heaven-born plan.

The test of great didactic skill
Is not to train the few
Whose active genius, tact, and will
Are always plain to view;
But he who takes an inert mind,

Housed in a sluggish frame,
And forms such man as God designed,
Deserves an honored name.

Like Sisyphus some ever roll
The same old round of things
Which dwarf the mind and starve the soul,
Until they long for wings
To fly from dull monotony,
Which carries in its train
That wreck of thought—Despondency—
Which preys on heart and brain.

The artist knows the colors best
That blend in harmony
With richest cloud-scenes, in the west,
That gild the sunset sky;
The minstrel knows what song to sing
To please the multitude;
His fingers deftly touch the strings
That yield response subdued
When weary soul would find relief
From sorrow's withering sigh,
Or when the heart is bowed with grief,
And tear-drops dew the eye;
But when the soul is full of joy,
How jubilant the strain
The tactful artist will employ
To please the heart and brain.

If those who toil in lowly spheres
Employ such artful ways
To charm the dull and listless ears
That such may sound their praise,
Why should the artist of the mind
Shrink from that noble aim
That seeks to elevate mankind,
And light a deathless flame!
Or why should he who shapes the lives
And destiny of man,
Be less exact than he who strives
From mercenary plan.

No instrument man ever made—
None ever can be found—
No matter when or where 'tis played,
Will yield so rich a sound
As that which falls from human tongue
When heart speaks unto heart,
Nor are its mysteries among
The hidden things of art;
A tyro on life's winding road
Reads understandingly
Each tone and word, each varied mode
The tongue and form portray.

Our heart's intents are from our looks
More plainly to be read,
Than thoughts expressed in printed books
Whose language oft seems dead,

Because it lacks a living form—
A voiceless, dull decree
That of itself has little charm
For youth's activity.

A potent charm of living light
Flows with resistless force,
Dispelling clouds of mental night
That meet its onward course,
When all the soul is centred in
The great and primal thought
That services which hearts would win,
With price can ne'er be bought.
Such service heaven alone repays
E'en though on earth 'tis done,
Its echoes last through endless days,
And dies but with the sun.
A mercenary soul must find
A more congenial field
Than that of training human mind
Wherein a soul's concealed,
If it would live out all the days
Allotted unto man,
And bask in all the genial rays
Revealed in God's great plan.

No lubrication of the nerves
Has ever yet been found,
For him who like a menial serves
Dull lesson's daily round;

But gnawing friction, stern and gaunt,
Tears flesh and brain away,
While ghosts nocturnal ever haunt
A soul with fell dismay,
Whose mercenary greed has led
Itself into a snare
That counts by scores its strangled dead,
Its hundreds, in despair.

He doubly lives who can forget
Himself and his own ease,
While toiling patiently to set
New gems in crowns he sees,
That may adorn some other head
Than that he calls his own,
And animate the germs wide spread
In seeds already sown.

———

To skim the surface of knowledge,
And seldom its root to reach,
Is a receipe one may offer
To direct "How Not To Teach."

NEEDS AND POWERS.

I KNOW of no profession
  'Mong profane or divine,
Excelling in its mission
  The power embraced in mine.

It reaches earth and heaven
  Through heart and soul of man,
It lives beyond the present—
  Eternity doth span.

Mind in its first formation,
  While in its plastic state,
Receives primal impressions
  Which make it vile or great.

When soil of thought is fertile
  And ready for the seeds,
It may bring precious fruitage,
  Or vile and noxious weeds.

No sower should be careless,
  For harvest much depends
Upon the well-selected seeds,
  With mental soil he blends.

OUR PROFESSION

If field be rich and mellow
And no good seed be sown,
With tangled mass of vileness
It will be overgrown,

And shield the deadly serpent,
The basilisk of sin,
That far exhales its pois'nous breath,
Then crawls its den within.

No atoms of pollution
In matter e'er was known,
So vile or so destructive
As soul by sin o'erthrown.

The vilest spot upon the earth,
Through sunshine, air, and rain,
May be transformed in ev'ry part
And purified again.

The fields where chaos reigned supreme
And Nature frowned aghast,
By patient-toil have fruitage borne
And blossomed fragrance cast.

The wreck of spheres by traction's laws
Hurled wildly into space,
May gather atoms round itself
And find some resting place

Where it may serve creation's end,
And 'mong the planets roll,
True to the laws of gravity
That marks its outer pole.

The mind and soul can never
Within themselves find rest,
When all the sin's pollutions
Are harbored in the breast.

Then sow good seed, brave teacher,
And deeply plant with care,
That both here and hereafter
Rich harvest it may bear.

The sowing may be silent—
It may be but a tear,
Its strength is in its purpose,
Its aim must be sincere.

It should not be a rite or creed,
But wider far than these,
It should encompass God and man,
Home and antipodes.

To learn the truths of science,
Know tables, books and charts,
To analyze the potent thrill
That fires all earnest hearts,

OUR PROFESSION

To revel in the mysteries
That lie deep in the earth,
To give the proper data
When planets had their birth,

To know the exact elements
That constitute the sun,
The causes why swift currents
Within the ocean run,

The ratio of the vapors
That color sunset skies,
Time's infinitesimal fraction
When planets set and rise,

To solve the problems of the air,
The secrets of the deep,
Are all intrinsic subjects
And worthy of our keep.

But these alone are worthless,
They need augmented force
To lead mind toward the fountain
From which it had its source.

They leave one vital question—
Development of man—
Without e'en crude solution,
Without a working plan.

They leave the mighty problem
Of Maker and the Made,
Devoid of any sequence,
Or any plan portrayed.

These are of greatest moment
To persons and to State,
Upon their wise adjustment
Must hang progression's fate.

Cold are the truths of science,
Lifeless their every plan,
Until in living presence,
They're crystalized in man.

As hidden truths are useless
And aid not human skill,
So slumber mighty forces
Through lack of human will.

To know the right is not enough,
It must be given power
Through culture of the heart and soul,
If it shall blessings shower.

To State, to manhood and to God
Must mind be wholly given,
Ere truth will shine a beacon light,
To illumine earth and heaven.

All things were made but to subserve
Man's powers to improve,
And beautify his being here
Through charity and love.

Power, gold, and wealth are agencies
Placed in a creature's hand
To serve an end, but not to rule,—
Obey, but not command.

As mind and soul matter surpass
And error flies from truth,
So should we train the nobler parts
Of plastic, trusting youth.

The sacred man by God ordained,
Links sinful earth with heaven,
But his success oft must depend
On how instruction's given.

The holy task of training mind
Is not a trivial thing,
Its influence lives, grows and expands
Till harvest it shall bring.

No task, to human hands assigned,
Excels in force and weight
The grave responsibilities
Of those who educate.

. Let knowledge of the sciences,
Skill in didactic art,
Power in the impulse of the soul
A knowledge to impart,

A love for God and human kind,
Forgetfulness of self,
A heart devoted to the cause
More than to worldly pelf,

Be given as a heritage
To those who fain would teach,
Then living truth shall flourish,
And all mankind shall reach.

———

There's an ebb and flow of sentiment
In educational tides,
Which oft discards some solid old facts,
And on wild new hobbies rides.
The educator of modern times
Must prove the false and the true,
Hold fast the worthy of the old,
Unprejudiced, test the new.

COURAGE AND FAITH.

COURAGE and Faith are of heavenly birth,
   Though sent down to our lowly earth
To cheer the heart of man ;
They are only strong when the human soul
Yields perfect trust and full control
   To heaven's benignant plan.

Nature expands when this God-sent pair
Finds a fertile heart that needs the care
   Of a messenger divine,
And permits their strength to succor give
That truth may grow and honor live
   To yield their fruit benign.

———

Who gives no sunshine from his soul
Must live in darkness ever,
For Nature scorns to such degree,
She blinds a sordid giver.

But he who scatters noble deeds,
And lives to bless mankind,
Shall see the beauties God reveals
To men with hearts refined.

INCOMPETENCE.

SOMETIMES our soul within us burns
    To see dark Ignorance aspire
To move toward light a mind that yearns
For knowledge that may lift it higher
    Upon the royal road of truth,
While every word and act and thought
Betrays an atmosphere so fraught
With lack of common sense and lore,
We plead for some almighty power
    To save from such our precious youth.

No ray of truth can ever shine
To beautify and make divine
The heart and mind of anxious soul,
When doubts and fears have full control
    Of him who knows he blindly leads.
If human minds and souls and hearts
May not command those who have arts
And power to waken, lead, inspire,
Then knowledge fails of her desire,
    And Ignorance on Wisdom feeds.

Let science, art, didactic skill,
Be guided by unyielding will
Born in some earnest, patient one
Whose heart glows like the summer sun
   And warms all by its ardent fire ;
Whose interest is so intense
It readily itself imprints
Upon the tender minds of youths,
Precepts and scientific truths
   Such as their yearning hearts desire.

Then there shall come a brighter day,
When darkness shall to light give way,
And Wisdom on her throne rejoice,
And speak with accent in her voice
   That charms and cheers a hungry mind.
Then, students, beauty shall receive
Instead of ashes that deceive,
Their days and nights of earnest toil,
Their struggles by the midnight oil
   Give recompense complete, refined.

FACT VERSUS FORM.

A S shadows are to material forms,
    As mists to the copious shower
As dead calms are to tornado storms
That in tropical region lower
So are educational falacies
That ignore and decry as naught
The value and power that ever lie
In the scope of original thought.

No smooth device with a soulless form
Should obscure the living thought;
It smothers the mind, destroys the charm
That comes to him who has wrought
To discover new truth, by a truth well known,
On which he may safely build,
Till his mental strength by use has grown
To a giant strong and skilled.

When thought is secure, the reason clear,
And the language to tell is pure,
Abridgement comes like a friend sincere,   .
For it cannot the mind obscure.
The wasted time on a form-clad task
Steals gems from youth's precious years,
Leaves a wreck on life's shore, we cannot mask
  With our sorrows and sighs and tears.

If what we have learned has given no power
To acquire what yet we must learn,
If all our past struggles leave not a dower
To which we may joyously turn
And feel that a strength within us is given
Through efforts already bestowed,
In vain have we lived, in vain have we striven,
Each task is the same weary load.

If task of to-day shall not lighten th' one
May come upon us to-morrow,
It is but a proof our work was ill done,
And bodes to us grief and sorrow.
Ev'ry effort of mind applied aright
Augments the mental perception,
For God aids the brave, and giveth a light
To shine away imperfection.

There's a magic power in a task well done,
There's a charm in solid reason,
There's a mighty force in a victory won,
Which an alert mind will seize on,
And with giant strength that is thus acquired
March on till the fields of science
And the zones of thought wherein man aspired
Shall be won by self-reliance.

INTEREST.

WHO has not seen the inert mind,
    Bowed down and sore oppressed,
Start into life, and vigor find
At touch of interest
Some sympathetic soul has shown,
By look in kindness given,
Or word whose accent, cadence, tone,
Gave joy akin to heaven?

No emanation from the heart
Has greater power to win,
Than that which lays aside all art
And quietly steps in
To soothe through sympathy, the cares
And sorrows, one by one,
Of timorous soul who scarcely dares
Go forward all alone,

But needs some word of magic power
To give him life and zest,
Some animating heart-given dower
Whose wealth is interest.
Few, few there are who know the force
That dormant lies in many a brain,
Who trace inertia to its source
Or see how mind o'er mind may reign.

MEMORY AND REASON.

WHO stores the mind with richest truth
  Gathered from sages of all lands, ·
May toil through days of sunny youth,
And on till Death gives his commands,
But fails to call to him the aid
Of Reason, Judgment, and Good Sense,
Will find himself at last dismayed
At smallness of his consequence.

The choicest gems must polish bear,
And metals must be purged from earth,
Before a lustre they can wear
That tells of their intrinsic worth.
The brain requires friction of thought,
Obtained through contact with the world,
With which may skillfully be wrought
The mental gems research unfurled.

Who builds alone on Memory
Will find he lacks a needed force
To fire and set the spirit free,
And move him onward in the course
That tends to lead him by a way
Whose goal is sure, complete success,
But wanting such, can but display
Chaotic mass of nothingness.

Let Memory and Reason wed,
Their product then may fully know
The food on which great minds are fed,
The founts from which great actions flow ;
Each holds its share of honored meed,
But each requires the other's aid
To stimulate the urgent need
By which great genius is displayed.

———

Many a brave resolution
Is formed on New Year's Day
To annihilate some vices
That on our morals prey;
But before the year is ended
They go so far astray
We find our lives are pursuing
The old, accustomed way.

THE DESIRABLE UNDEFINED.

I have often thought there's a power
  Unknown to science or art,
That opens and closes the portals
That lead to the human heart.

I have learned there's a secret something
That remains yet undefined,
That touches the springs and pulleys
That open the human mind.

I have watched the glow of faces,
As a light from this occult source
Has touched some inert nature
With an energizing force.

The effect was so magnetic,
It seemed like creative skill
From the hand of the Great Master,
To give passive being *will.*

Sometimes its power seemed but presence,
Sometimes, a soft, mild tone,
Sometimes, a look of decision,
Ofttimes, from a source unknown.

There's a something wrapped in th' nature
Of those most adapted to teach
That charms and holds the attention
Of those whom its powers reach.

There's a sound from some vibration
Within the human voice
That arouses the latent spirit
And makes the soul rejoice.

Its tone has a magic power
Whereby the heart is impressed
With the weight of its noble mission
And unselfish interest.

There's a mystic charm most winsome
In th' glance of a speaking eye
Whose light shines in dark recesses
And explores them in passing by.

It illumines the page of the student
As his soul warms by its fire,
And stirs him to greater action,
And lifts aspirations higher.

Every word and look and action
Has weight on trustful youth,
That needs no sage to interpret
Or explain its vital truth.

They are fully comprehended
Through the instinct, every one,
And need no labored searching
In a massive lexicon.

Some call this power attraction,
Some term it affinity,
But all recognize its existence
And wonderful potency.

There's also a power of repulsion
That breathes with abated breath,
Whose presence is best betokened
By ominous signs of death.

No word has an inspiration,
No look has a sign of cheer,
Each act reveals that a burden
Must be borne in sorrow and fear.

The wrecks that are made by its presence
Have filled almshouses and jails
With the deepest of lamentations,
The saddest of human wails.

A selfish, terrible monster
That drives away honor and truth
Is the cold-blooded fiend Repulsion,
The destroyer of tender youth.

The sea in its frenzy and fury,
When lashed by the wintry gales
Casts on the rocks its vessels
Bereft of their spars and sails;

The path of the fierce tornado,
Overstrewn with wild debris
Of fallen habitations
And uprooted forest tree;

The wreck of a world of matter
That transforms revolving spheres,
Which have gathered all their greatness
Through the lapse of a million years;

The snow-clad mountain terror—
The fearful avalanche—
Whose thunders are heard in valleys
Where imploring faces blanch;

The mouth of a raging Etna
With its stifling breath of fire,
Wherein the pride of a city
In a moment may expire;

The trembling of the mountains
When an earthquake passes by,
And the terror of the people
Struck dumb in their agony ;

The rage of a foaming torrent,
After the bursting cloud
Has poured its liquid fury
In destruction wild and loud;

Are but the potent protests
Of Nature's elements
Against some ill arrangement
That brings them discontents.

But these in separate actions,
Or in forces all combined,
Leave not so sad a ruin
As the wreck of one human mind.

The voice, the eye, and the manner
Are all unlocked by a key
That has for its great attraction
A confiding sympathy.

The knowledge of books is essential
To those who youth would guide,
But the grace of earnest endeavor
Excels all else beside.

Truth in its plainness is beauty,
Science itself is a charm,
But the frown of a tyrant tutor
Puts both in constant alarm.

To receive a healthful impression,
Mind must be free from fear,
Will must be held by attraction,
Soul, by a soul sincere.

———

MIRRORS.

SOME persons in mind are but mirrors
   Reflecting what others have thought,
That make no original errors,
They are only able to quote.
You may ask their opinion on matters
That pertain to affairs of the day,
Their minds are but shreds and tatters
Of what all their neighbors say.

We respect the man who is careful
With others his mind to compare,
But who of himself is not fearful
His honest opinion to share
With men, when some public measure
Upon the State has been thrown,—
Who proves his mind a rich treasure
He uses and calls his own.

MANY.

MANY a grand ambition
        Had birth and died in a day,
From lack of vigorous nursing
To keep it from decay.

Many a hope has faded
And sunk in deepest despair,
Through lack of careful pruning
That fruitage it might bear.

Many a mind is ruined
And becomes chaotic mass,
Through want of systematic
Training in the class.

Many a song of sweetness
Has lost its harmony,
Because at its beginning
It had not the proper key.

Many a field most fertile
Bears vile and noxious weeds,
Through failure of the tiller
To sow some worthy seeds.

Many a flower of beauty
And sweetness blooms unseen,
And dies in its seclusion
On a bed of mossy green.

Better to have no talent,
No excellence to give,
Than permit vice to destroy
The talent we may have.

———

No dam can restrain the water
When leaks receive no care,
When the tempest in wild fury
Doth chafe and gnaw and tear,
And no hand is raised to succor,
No effort to repair,
Till the torrent bursts in fury
And fills us with despair.
'Tis too late then for repining,
Too late, for work or prayer.

DUTY DONE.

A duty done is victory won,
　　E'en though in the doing,
Efforts may fail to bring avail
　　In lines we are pursuing.

Nothing is lost whate'er the cost,
　　When efforts made are noble,
Beyond the sky acts never die,
　　And honor's crown is double.

Right cannot fail, but must prevail,
　　If noble be the motive;
Heaven is nigher if we aspire
　　With hearts sincere and votive.

Much strength we gain when we maintain
　　A truth for truth's sake solely;
A mighty power guides effort's hour
　　And stamps its cause as holy.

If honest heart act well its part,
　　And ask the aid of heaven
Its feeblest word will be so heard
　　That succor will be given.

It matters not how low our lot
  We rise by honest trial;
No effort made for needed aid
  E'er met complete denial.

The soul expands when it demands
  A right for self and others,
And darkest night has ray of light
  For honest helpful brothers.

A noble soul spurns the control
  Would bind in servile fetters;
No chains can bind God-given mind
  Inspired by love and letters.

An earnest will can ne'er be still
  Though oft its hopes be baffled,
It will succeed though victims bleed
  And die upon the scaffold.

Loud shout and sing, "Crown Effort King,"
  And let the watchword be
This earnest prayer heard everywhere,
  "God and Humanity."

A duty done is victory won,
  For strength comes by the doing;
There's no retreat, there's no defeat,
  If right we are pursuing.

THE SENSES.

THE EYE.

SOME eyes are trained to scan large field
  Till instantaneous glance may yield
A knowledge full and plenty;
While others keep a narrow ken
And view the ways of active men
  With satisfaction scanty.

The optic nerve has power so keen,
That ev'ry object by it seen
  Is stamped upon the brain;
But they of sluggish mental mold
No vivid photograph will hold,
  And scarce a scene retain.

THE EAR.

The tympanum with perfect drum
Hears not the sound when armies come
  With clarion notes and song,
Unless its stimulated nerve
Has fully learned to humbly serve
  In stations which belong

To those which God designed should live
For special duties, He might give
　　To move mankind along
Upon the road toward perfect man,
That He might thus reveal His plan,
　　And happiness prolong.

THE TONGUE.

The power that lies in perfect speech
Dwells with the few who only reach
　　That art through toil and care;
A faulty tongue perverts the ear,
Destroys the sense, augments the fear,
　　And feeds on empty air.

A nation's destinies have hung
Upon the influence of a tongue
　　Whose magic eloquence
Has swayed the thoughts of men, whose word
Was mightier than the glittering sword
　　Of armies most immense.

THE HAND.

The manual touch when guided by
The magic power of sympathy
　　That animates the soul,
May lead to fields of cultured art
And cast an influence on the heart
　　May through all ages roll.

The canvass and the stone may speak
To more than Roman and to Greek
   Though in a foreign land;
They show the might of cultured skill
Directed by an iron will
   That guides a master's hand.

THE NOSE.

The perfumed fields of blooming May,
The evening scent of new-mown hay
   Touch nerve olfactory,
And carry to the thoughtful brain
Loved memories of a long-past train
   That once was full of glee.

Though flowers to-day are choice and rare,
In colors they may well compare
   With richest hues we meet;
They lack the charm that gave them power
Since past is youth's entrancing hour
   Their fragrance seems less sweet.

COMBINED INFLUENCE.

Five roads lead to the human brain
And through these roads all must obtain
   The commerce of all lore;
No thought can enter mental port
Of any kind or any sort,
   Of modern days or yore,

Except such as a tariff pays
To pass these honored, great highways
  Which lead to eminence,
And follow closely every nerve
Which God designed should truly serve
  Each mind of consequence.

———

Perhaps that star in yonder sky,
May be my dwelling place on high,
  When life on earth is done;
At eventide I love to gaze
Upon its soft reflected rays,
  When silent and alone.

Its brightness charms and draws my soul,
By some mysterious, strong control
  I cannot well explain,
Unless it be within it dwell
The friends of earth I loved so well,
  Who could not here remain.

SOUL SPEAKS TO SOUL.

SOUL speaks to soul, eye speaks to eye,
  And mind by mind is read;
The heart bounds in sweet ecstasy
Whene'er a light is shed,
That shines to illume a cherished thought
That seemed to dwell alone,
But on through years has nobly sought
To solve some truth unknown.

The living truth that seemeth dead,
Needs but a kindred touch
To resurrect thought's vital thread,
And give it influence, such
As breaks the bands of fettered mind,
And sunders thraldom's chains,
Spreads benefactions, pure, refined,
Where ignorance now reigns.

Magnetic touch of spark divine,
Speak to the inert soul,
Let light from out the darkness shine,
And truth her page unroll;
Speak to the minds that waiting, starve,
And give them power to see,
That he who patiently will serve
Shall win the victory.

OUR BATTLEFIELD.

[Written for an entertainment given by the Fife and Drum
Corps (36 uniformed members) of the Third Ward Grammar
School of Long Island City, of which the writer is Principal.]

THERE are fields of martial glory
    Where the slain are ne'er bemoaned;
There are victories though silent,
    Where grim monarchs are dethroned;
There are scenes of strife and foray
    Where gigantic forces strive
For the mastery and triumph
    Of the ends for which they live.

There are forces more puissant
    Than ten million armed men,
There are banners that are emblems
    Of the mighty tongue and pen,
That reflect upon their blazon
    Honest purpose grand and true,
Such as never graced the victors
    Of Sedan and Waterloo.

There are weapons in these contests
    Keener than the Damask blade,
There are metals of such temper
    As no crucible e'er made;
For the dross must be extracted
    In the furnace of the soul
Till no refuse or pollution
    Shall defile the perfect whole.

Though this army counts its millions,
    Each must face alone the foe,
Each must bring a special weapon,
    Each must strike himself the blow
That shall free him from the shackles
    Of that despot and his train,
Who with ignorance and vices
    Would destroy the heart and brain.

Our true sword is Education
    And grim Ignorance our foe;
We are battling with our passions,
    And our spirits are aglow
With a full determination
    To accept the proven truth
That the days of precious seed-time,
    Are the sunny days of youth.

Day by day the contest rages
    And each task that's daily done,
Brings a soothing satisfaction
    That another victory's won.

Thus the strength we gain in action
    Aids in each succeeding strife,
To make the struggles lighter
    In the battles of our life.

There are avenues and byways
    Which lead into the heart,
Whose intricate environments
    Require the highest art
To tell what inspiration
    Shall touch a dormant mind,
And fire it with a living zeal
    For a station more refined.

It is only voice of music
    That speaks universal tongue;
It matters not in what accent
    A sweet melody is sung,
It will find responsive feelings
    Which will aptly understand
Though it be of unknown measure
    And sung in a foreign land.

We come with our martial music,
    With our noisy fife and drum
To inspire the weak and weary,
    To open the mouths of the dumb,
To train our every emotion
    For a better sphere in life,
To enjoy for the passing moment
    The sound of the drum and fife.

We hope our notes may be peaceful
    And free from carnage of war;
We would bind up the broken hearted
    And cover the wound and scar,
But should foe our country menace
    And refuse to be just and calm,
We would sound aloud the tocsin
    And march to defend Uncle Sam.

———

To plant an intellectual seed
And guard its growth from noxious weed,
That it may fruitage bear,
Is solace more, a thousand fold,
Than hoarding bonds and stocks and gold,
Or sporting jewels rare.

GOOD HABITS.

A silent force marks out the course
   Of every man and woman,
No matter what may be the lot
Of creatures that are human,

The end attained is ever gained
By means so strange and hidden,
We call it luck, instead of pluck,
Or fate by fairies bidden.

The human eye cannot descry
All workings of the brain;
At silent night, it gains a might
Which bears a mental train

Whose lucid glow may thrones o'erthrow,
Or bid new nations rise,
May prove some plan whereby proud man
May ransack earth and skies.

Think not such power a fairy's dower,
Or influence from some star,
It did not spring from anything
Beyond what mortals are.

To man is given the keys of heaven
If they be rightly used;
No being born but must be shorn
If blessings are abused.

Keep well the trust!   Guard it we must,
From in and outward foes,
Strength will be gained, might be attained
By efforts to oppose

The secret vice that doth entice
To ruin and despair;
But he who will hath power to kill
Such vice within its lair.

Let habits grand the life command
And Eden is regained;
No future bliss need surpass this
If habits are unstained.

Let smiling face your presence grace
And earth will smile on you,
Let from the tongue a song be sung,
Its echo will be true,

And sing again the same refrain
Upon the selfsame key,
Till airs elate, reverberate,
Heaven's sweetest minstrelsy.

If we extend a hand to friend
Who needs a brother's care,
Though it may hold no purse of gold
The act he will revere.

Scarce do we know whence comes the glow
That duty done e'er gives,
Its altar-fire cannot expire—
Here and hereafter lives.

Such habits then, for gods and men,
Are but the means whereby
They may prepare to gain their share
To mansions in the sky.

Sing then a song, its notes prolong,
In praise of Habit's power;
Let custom be from evil free
And it will blessings shower.

EVIL HABITS.

HOW habit grows no one e'er knows,
   And yet he is a giant
That has a will and subtle skill
That never yet was pliant.

'Tis very plain that he has slain
More than the sword and spear,
With wily art he charms the heart
And quells the greatest fear.

His artful eye is wondrous sly
And has bewitching glance,
Where'er he moves his victim loves
To see his powers advance.

He makes no noise 'mong girls and boys
Whom he would call his own,
His spell is cast, he holds them fast
Till they are overthrown.

When this is done the field is won,
And they are all his own,
He heeds no cry, no choking sigh,
No plea, no prayer, no groan.

If you would be forever free
From tyrant so severe,
Watch every thought before you're caught,
For he is hovering near.

Your every word guard with the sword
Of truth, which never fails,
Its honor's sung in every tongue,
Its power e'er prevails.

Act well your part, and keep your heart
Free from the tares he sows,
For at the end like traitor friend
He leaves you with your woes.

Thus Habit mars with wounds and scars
The favored of our race,
Transforms the mind that God designed
Should be the dwelling place

Of noble thought with heaven fraught
Into a sterile plain,
Whose atmosphere is dank and drear—
A wild chaotic brain.

Man scarce may be entirely free
From wiles and tricks and snares,
Whose stealthy forms and subtle charms
Approach us unawares.

Our eyes are blind or not inclined
To see that powerful hand,
That silently, yet forcibly
Gives us its strong command.

———

LIFE'S EMERGENCIES.

HOW strangely dark are the vapors
    That sometimes obscure the way,
Ere the light of truth advances
    To the noon of a perfect day.

As the unforeseen approaches
    In stealth from ambushed retreat,
The mettle of soul is summoned
    Its emergencies to meet.

To shrink by its sudden coming,
    To surrender our control
Without a struggle for vantage,
    Betrays a weakness of soul.

The conflicts with emergencies
    We meet in our daily call,
Give strength or death to moral worth
    As we conquer them or fall.

To meet at once with valor true
   The attack from an ambuscade,
In moral strife, or bloody war,
   Hath many·a hero made.

Who has not trained himself to meet
   The vicissitudes that arise
Upon the course of life's stern race,
   Must fail to secure its prize.

———

To hold a pessimistic view,
And see the world as darkly " blue,"
And feel mankind is false, untrue,
   Is not a just conclusion;
But Truth demands that Hope shall wear
No false rose in her silken hair,
To hide Deceit, Fraud, and Despair,
   That feed on wild Delusion.

STRAND DESPAIR.

THE wrecks that lie on Strand Despair,
　　Should serve as buoys on life's stern seas
To guide the voyager safely, where
He may escape the tides and breeze
That drive to whirlpools, bars, and rocks,
Where human vessels oft impinge
And leave a ruin that but mocks
The pleadings of persuasion's hinge.

An idle mind, companions base,
A shrinking from a duty known,
A sly deceit, a brazen face,
A lying tongue, a sullen tone,
Lead toward a wreck on Strand Despair,
And none but self can move the helm
To change the course for scenes more fair,
To save from storms that overwhelm.

INDULGENCE.

A N alarm is sounding through the land
. That tells of a stronger foe
Than that which marched on Lexington,
To strike a fatal blow
At the liberties our sires did claim
For themselves and all mankind,
For this foe is a product of deceit.
And sophistry combined.

Its victims fall by the smiling ways
Of a charmed environment
That lures him on to neglect and sin,
And to final banishment
Of the vital spark of an earnest man,
And all that is noble and true,
To the effete round of nothingness
Which honor and strength will subdue.

No Spartan Helen of beauty and fame,
No mermaid with winsome face,
No Siren that sings an alluring song,
No Pandora in her grace,
Can soothe and charm to destruction's retreat,
Like the foe that robs of power
To meet the needs of life's true aim,
The requirements of each hour.

Might sway the poise from adjustment,
    And his judgment go astray,
Through the frailties of his nature—
    Imperfect humanity

The Infallible in knowledge,
    Whose true balance never swerves,
Knows every man's Gethsemane,
    And the merit he deserves.
He will not ask figs of the thorns;
    Of talents will not demand
A greater increase than is just
    From a faithful steward's hand.
Feeling the weight of the mission
    Incumbent upon our care;
Searching the heart's deep recesses
    That vice may not shelter there;
Working courageously onward
    The truth and right to defend;
And asking a perfect guidance,
    We calmly welcome the end.